REFLEXIVE
CONVERSATIONS

JOHN EVERETT BUTTON

authorHOUSE®

AuthorHouse™
1663 Liberty Drive
Bloomington, IN 47403
www.authorhouse.com
Phone: 1-800-839-8640

First published by AuthorHouse 7/15/2010

ISBN: 978-1-4490-9322-8 (e)
ISBN: 978-1-4490-9321-1 (sc)
ISBN: 978-1-4520-6006-4(hc)

Library of Congress Control Number:

Printed in the United States of America

This book is printed on acid-free paper.

ACKNOWLEDGEMENTS

I have been incredibly fortunate to have had the support of many individuals in writing this book. Without their help and encouragement, it would have been impossible, and I would like to thank them: Beth Klim for her undivided encouragement and editorial support; Joe Addams for his absolutely wonderful formatting of my text; Brian Zuckerman for his beautiful work on the front cover; Michael Friedman for his feedback on earlier drafts and his undying support of my writing; Dr. Michael Veber for being a trusted friend and advisor; The Daugherty Family for supporting my writing when I needed it most; and of course my very own family, who have helped me throughout this entire journey.

REFLEXIVE

CONVERSATIONS

CONTENTS

INTRODUCTION

REFLEXIVE CONVERSATIONS

Reflexive Conversations (*RC*) is an epic poem, which tells the tragic tale of the Devil's odyssey to hell as told in three separate books or "conversations" (*Reflexive Conversations I, II,* and *III*). The word 'reflexive' means, according to Webster, something that is "directed or turned back on itself." For example, consider the German reflexive verb "sich waschen" meaning "to wash oneself." In this case, the verb's action comes back to the person. *RC* is 'reflexive' in exactly this sense; the conversations refer back to the main speaker, the Devil. Initially, the word "conversation" is a bit misleading, suggesting a series of dialogues. Conversely, *RC* is better described as a series of monologues where the Devil is telling his story to someone else. However, there is a real sense in which the Devil is talking with himself, ultimately taking himself back through his own journey.

In addition, the poem is "reflexive" in several less obvious ways. First, the word 'reflexive' is used to represent something spontaneous or elicited automatically. All the "conversations" in *RC I, II,* and *III* are brought about in some spontaneous manner. Secondly, the poem is written largely in the first person, to force the reader to experience the dialog, as though they were retelling their own story. In this way, the poem fosters a unique individual connection between the reader and the protagonist. Lastly, each book is *reflexive* in itself "reflecting" on the prior "conversations." Each book contains a different conversation, with a different person, during a different time. Each "conversation" can be read and understood by itself; however, by combining the books the reader will uncover the emergence of a single story illuminating their understanding of the entire work.

In *RC* the dramatic goal for the reader is to reach an unequivocal level of empathy and catharsis. Given the first-person reading of *RC*, many people may initially find it hard to identify with the Devil. Some individuals may find themselves automatically repulsed by any kind or sympathetic words supporting such a controversial figure and symbol. Despite these understandable prejudices, it should be clearly stated that *RC* is not interested or invested in any theological entity. *RC*'s protagonist is a secular character who traverses a Judeo-Christian landscape. Thus, a brief explanation of the book's protagonist is necessary.

THE DEVIL AND FREE WILL

The Devil of *Reflexive Conversations* is described in a largely non-traditional sense--as an ordinary man who couldn't get to heaven (The Great Beyond). While eliminating several prominent traditional characteristics (e.g. the devil is a fallen *angel* who is evil, diabolical, a tempter, has claws and wings, etc.), the theological understanding of the devil as one who fails to be with God in heaven is retained resulting in a character that is supremely identifiable with tragedy and loss. This eternal disbarment from heaven and eternal bliss make him the ideal candidate to play the archetypal role of loss and suffering. Caught amongst a sudden flood of intense memories of his lost love, he is sent into a fateful journey where he is led through many changes of fortune, searching for a sanctuary from the heartache he has endured.

In this poem, the devil is manifested as a romantic character who wanders the world by foot and sail. This characteristic is bolstered by the etymology of the word 'Satan' which is synonymous with 'Devil.' Job 1:7 in the Old Testament provides an alternative understanding in Hebrew of 'Satan.' When God asks him from where he came, Satan responds, "From wandering (mi'šuṭ) about the earth and walking around on it." The root šuṭ signifies wandering on foot or sailing. Thus, 'Satan' is understood in the broad sense of being one who is a wanderer. After he commits his great sin (eating from the Tree of Life), he finds himself eternally living out his judgment. 'Sin' used in this context is not referring to a moral wrong, but rather an eudaimonistic error. In the biblical Hebrew, the generic word for 'sin' is *het*, which means "to err or miss the mark or target." In this sense, the Devil "misses the mark" for fulfilling his life, because he is eternally banned from heaven due to his inability to overcome the loss of his lover.

To make matters worse, the Devil learns that our lives are in fact pre-determined by "fateful forces" around us. Furthermore, he discovers that to truly fulfill oneself and be happy one must have desires which *will* be satisfied while living out their fate. The Devil ascertains that achieving one's eudaimonistic end is a matter of luck; one can only hope that their fate will align with their innate desires and hopes. If the stars have aligned, then one has fulfilled their life and is free; otherwise, the person's life has missed the mark and, consequently, they have sinned. Thus, *RC* is a loosely compatibilist approach to tragedy.

Compatibilism is the philosophical view that free will and determinism are compatible, and that they are *not* logically inconsistent. For this poem, the protagonist's actions are determined and caused by factors outside his control (his inherited traits and environment). For example, his life can still "hit the mark" and he can be free of tragic suffering if his environment happens to coincide with his desires. One way of visualizing this concept of life is to picture a man sitting in a chair in the middle of a room. Further suppose the man has chosen, because it satisfies him, to sit in this chair and stay inside this room. However, unbeknownst to the sitting man, the room's door, which is closed, is also locked on the outside and the man couldn't leave the room if he wanted to. Although in some basic sense, he is determined to be in the room, he has chosen to stay in that room. His natural desire to stay in the room is consistent with the circumstances of his environment, thus he is fulfilled and free. As it is true for most individuals in life, the Devil's character isn't as fortunate as the man who chose to stay in the room.

RC's setting and philosophical framework represents that of which we all wander in. The Devil, represents every person's search for happiness; the trials and tribulations which cause us to "miss our target," the searching for purpose and fulfillment we all find ourselves in, and the internal redemption which we hope to eventually find; in ourselves; in our children; in tomorrow; in the afterlife. The Devil represents a part of us all.

I

REFLEXIVE CONVERSATIONS

I. REFLEXIVE CONVERSATIONS

Raten…no, riet

The Devil sits mastering this new rhyme
With his Piano concerto 21
On Repeat

No evil inside
Just music, books, and rose-pedaled wine
Interested in the beauty of love,
Things good natured and fine

Different mediums line his tall shelves:
Screw-tape tragedies and string symphonies
Aged wines and dried tobacco leaves
Egg-based paints and boar-haired brushes
Small black hammers and thin chisels

Incense burns beside him in a suspended golden censer:
Smoke slowly tumbles upward
Drifting blindly through the darkness
And into the sunlight

David and Adonis stand silently in pillars of light–

Looking up into their distant gazes,
He sees himself
Forever trapped in youth and beauty

Without rising from his throne
He pours himself a full glass of a blush-red wine
From a tall crystal carafe beside him
Poise and punctilio disappear with each sip

I will be sitting here until these statues turn to dust
And the walls of this palace collapse into sand
I will be watching when the stars fade from the sky
And the only stirring in the universe is my eyes

You can't see the thorns tethered to my heart
Or the cancer that consumed my mortal soul
There is nothing for you to love about my life
For my fate is not that of a hero

He knew I was prepared to leave, to be as great as he
I had high hopes of chiseling myself into the rock of history
So that I too, like his beloved statues, would take a legendary
    form

A great pale horse appeared at the foot of the palace steps
Prepared to carry me as a conqueror
Before every tribe, tongue, and nation

Concern spread over his face
For he feared that something terrible lurked
Not behind me, but before me

To himself he whispered,

Behold a pale horse
His name that sat on him was Death
And Hell followed with him

As I turned towards the great ghostly horse
He interrupted my movement and said

Before you leave, you must know the truth of this throne,
For I fear my fate will become your own

And with that he closed his book

II. THE BEGINNING

His empty gaze shifted past me across the marble floor and into
  some lively memory

He closed his eyes and looked inward:
Visions bloomed from deep within the soft valves of his heart

He became a medium, commiserating with his past self
As he began to speak in a soft certainty

I fell from the gates of heaven
Without hate and without fear
Thinking of a woman whom I loved so dear

I was thrown back into the world
Left to bask forever in Purgatory
Not knowing that a long journey awaited me

I was welcomed again by my lover
And at my long journeys end
Fate decided that I should lose her again

I will tell you all that I remember
For your life is intertwined with mine

REFLEXIVE CONVERSATIONS

III. AUGURIES OF PURGATORY

I had come to the end of my life
And stood at the edge of the world
Peering down into the emptiness just beyond my feet:

> An eternal descent into darkness

Birds flew off, never to return
Distant rivers rushed off the land
Tuffs of long-stemmed grass bowed over the edge as the wind
swept past,

> And there I stood at the very end of earth, before God's
> Great Beyond:

Huge shifting clouds consumed in burning light,
Spinning, churning into each other,
Absorbing the atmosphere; consuming all the air that blew past
me

I had no fear, though, for faith filled my lungs,
Giving courage to my limbs to walk across the bottomless abyss
And into the Great Beyond

As I rested my left foot upon the emptiness before me,
(Like a blind man stepping onto a bridge)
All the faith and heavenly light could not calm
A sudden flood of desperate memories;

> Faith could not purge my memories of my forgotten Love
> lost

And as before, I surrendered and fell
Watching the bright clouds race away from me
Lost in the feeling of 'forever'

(Unconscious)

IV. THE CALM SEA

(Conscious)

The world is quietly circling around
As I awaken to the gentle slapping of the deep blue
That surrounds me

A benevolent raft, tied with vine
Settles with the jealous current
Together we drift west, following a passing sun

Lonely clouds move above the calm uncharted water

In a passing moment, I begin to consider
The spots and wrinkles that have appeared on my hands;
A natural tension curls my fingers slightly

To the vast Calm Sea I utter:

Oh, how quickly Time consumes us

The Calm Sea ignores my utterance
And continues me past like a silent chauffeur

So I just sit, balancing my forearms on my knees,
Resting; waiting until the gravity of the world
Gets tired of such a burden

REFLEXIVE CONVERSATIONS

V. MY SIRENS

Flashes of golden light caught my tired eyes
Songs of sympathy began to strike my tender ears
Forcing my body to the edge of my small wooden vessel,
Unsure of what was approaching:

Three women with long golden hair emerged from the sea,
Perched on the crest of an islet:
Two columns of rock standing firmly upon the calm water
Merging together into an open archway

Waves of harmonious falsetto surrounded me
Their long golden hair flashed in the sun
I began to frantically paddle with my hands
Submitting to the Siren's calls

As I approached the mouth of the islet's hallow archway
I looked up to see figures of the most tempting and lustful design
High up, looking off into the distance
Holding endless notes in harmony together

I fell into my own illusion
Of climbing up the islet's steep columns
And resting beside them
In eternal awe

Their voices penetrated my mind
Fish-eyed and vulnerable I began to sing,
Thoughtlessly and without strain,
A song which I had never known:

(Music)

"I've been lost for a long, long time
Searching all the seas
For a place that's pure and rich with cures
For all the things I don't need

She lured my soul with her golden hair
I answered "what do you need?"
I found myself on a distant land
In the middle of the sea

(Refrain)

    I know, I know
    This trip won't be easy
    And I know, I know
    It's hard to please me
    But if I wait, then I might find...

The sirens want me, cause I'm so weak
They know I'll never leave
Their beauty presses me like a wrecking ball
Nothing else can I see
She's got a golden comb for her golden hair
She's got a song to sing
I'll be here for the rest of my entire life
Lost in her melody

(Refrain)

    I know, I know
    I'm drifting away
    I know, I know
    There's nothing to say
    But if I wait, then I might find...

I'll be here for the rest of my entire life
Lost in her melody
She'll have me till I'm dead and gone
But at least I'll be free…"

(End)
The siren's voices were now behind me and the illusion vanished
I found myself at the end of the damp archway,
Floating into warm afternoon light
Towards the glowing sands of an long narrow island

The kind current carried me away from the sirens
And onto the crest of a wave
That quickly rolled me into its funnel
And delivered me onto the island's warm sands

REFLEXIVE CONVERSATIONS

VI. MELON COLONY

I'll play you something from Melon Colony,
The wanderers' commune on the Island of Purgatory,
That place between death and eternity;
A land of forgotten memories

I washed onto a most distant resort of the deeply isolated
Who wait, with spent, day-dreamt eyes, for feelings that will
    abide
I felt my worry escape me, suspended in a warm passing
    breeze,
Hanging around like a wandering orchestrated piece

Waves crashed on the beach
Carrying in the drifters,
Look like sun-tanned natives
From time spent on long rafts,
Laid out,
Asleep,
Surrounded by a sea's deeply unconscious waters
Dreaming of their past;
Lamenting their own fall before the Great Beyond

Palm trees line the edge of the golden sand
Hunched over and silent

Lying along the beach
Few desert the comforting sand
Exposed to the warmth that wraps their olive-skinned bodies
And slows the time

Hollow wooden wind chimes
Quiet hymns of tired voices
Nylon string guitars

REFLEXIVE CONVERSATIONS

There's a straw-roofed bamboo bar
Where many are seen drinking
And smoking Melon Colony cigars:

Bar flies speaking their minds
Homeless and those lost of heart, and others;
Pearl and Mirror Queens, forever waiting for the date
who's late

The Melon Colony is a hidden haven; a little Havana

But after a short while
I looked at those around me,
And began to consider my existence
And the overwhelming emptiness that filled it

My romantic amnesia began to fade
My veil of comfort fell away;
I longed to be alone in quiet mourning

As the sun retreated away,
Dividing night from day,
The stars became clearer,
And the hopes held within for tomorrow,
Followed me into my dreams

VII. THE DRUNKEN COUPLE

Day came like an obedient tearful slave;
A gentle rain awoke me
The clouds soon dissolved and the sands radiated,
But few of the olive-skinned people took notice

    Waves of blue
    Crash along the shore

Murmuring throughout the night deprived me of any rest:

A drunken couple stumbled onto the beach
With his arm draped around her, they leaned against each other,
Balancing across the dark dimpled sands
Blindly crashing down beside me

While they shared a mango, I heard the woman whisper close to
    his ear:

    "...the founders of Melon Colony:

    An attractive young couple,
    They were first on the island,
    Living on this beach
    Leaving behind stories of their Genesis:

        The couple awoke beside each other,
        Awakening from dreams of nothing
        Rising together, they stood upon barren soil;
        A garden sprung up all around them

        Humble trees began to stretch their branches
        Tiny plants and flowers sprouted from the soil
        Strange little lizards scurried up trees
        Eggs hatched and birds flew out

REFLEXIVE CONVERSATIONS

They built a house and enclosed it with a golden gate
But curiosity led them through the garden,
Over the Gate, and to the other side;
The young couple fled the Great Garden forever

The Garden was said to have never been found again..."

The island's surrounding jungle seemed to call out to me
To leave Melon Colony and search for this strange paradise

VIII. IN SEARCH OF THE GARDEN OF EDEN

I left the beach and moved into the jungle
Following the beaten path said to be of great men
It wandered and weaved like an ancient river bed,
Becoming increasingly narrow
And disappearing
Among the
Gro
wt
h

Green growth matured with each step
The tangled trees and vines devoured the light
Only streams of day poked through the thick mist
Providing short glimpses of what was before me

I pushed overgrown palms (like elephant ears)
Away from my face
I marched past the low-lying drip-tipped leaves;
Beads of moisture rolled down their smooth green spines

Trees were giant wooden towers
With rich umbrella crowns
I swung from hanging vines
Over the trees' large exposed roots

The jungle closed in behind me as I passed through
Erasing any tracks I may have left
Discovering a large knife partially buried in the thin forest soil
I slashed through the debris before me with little effect

After some time I came to a narrow ravine
That split across the entire island
Looking over the steep edge I could see rushing water
Racing through the channel

Walking along the ravine's edge,
I found a rotting tree which had fallen between both sides,
Half of its roots ripped from the earth,
Branching into the air

The tree's trunk extended across the ravine
Just shy of the other side
I mounted the tree's back and crawled,
Slowly shifting along like a caterpillar

    Bark flaked off around me
    Fluttering down into the loud water

The wood began to feel soft and moist on my hands
As I neared the end, the trunk began to bob up and down
The old tree began to whine
Its wood popping and whistling

The tree's whining grew louder

I rose to my feet—
Tossed the knife onto the land—
Squatted—
And leapt

    The trunk broke away
    Falling into the calling water

Crashing against the ravine's wall,
I clung to course tree roots protruding from the ravine's wall
My hands burned as I hung there struggling up the side
And pulling myself onto the land

Looking back across the gorge I realized:
A new impasse;
I could not return, so I continued forward
Into the jungle

It became alive; a vast system of consciousness

REFLEXIVE CONVERSATIONS

IX. THE GARDEN OF EDEN

I pushed aside a heavy palm leaf
And was confronted by a vibrant overgrown garden of unnatural
   birth
Enclosed by a fallen golden gate

Water poured over the sides of a granite fountain
Feeding a steady stream that flowed beside me
The word "Pishon" was etched into its stone

     I was astounded by the garden's undisturbed evolution

A silver scaled serpent with smooth black eyes
Slithered along the short banks of the stream
Swallowing a two-headed frog perched on a black lily

In the dark-wooded trees of the garden
Rested enormous lizards across the sturdy branches,
With their tails swaying freely beneath them

Passing the fountain's green-checkered ivy
I heard the distant hard flapping of an ancient bird
Moving over the tops of the trees

     A massive shadow glided past

Through the shining lines of a triangular spider web,
I could see a hundred praying mantises,
On a pew of raised earth in stiff praise

     A pink wall of giant camellia flowers blocked further sight

An open roar bellowed from the other side of the garden–
Sent tremors like gentle waves under my feet and up the trees
   trunks,
Scattering tiny red-striped birds into flight

As I pushed past the bright flower heads
I found myself at the foot of a white mansion
Each of its three floors had a terrace that tightly wrapped the
house

The front doors were partially open,
Revealing a dark redwood twin staircase,
A small walkway snaked beneath the staircases into a bright
open room

I slowly entered

Cat-sized monkeys with large round eyes and long striped tails
roamed the interior,
Crawling in and out of the holes and cracks in the old roof
Pausing to watch me

Through the small almond-shaped passage between the twin
staircase,
Was a large empty room with no opposing wall
Leaving it completely open to the outside

The room merged with a long flight of stairs that led down
To a large stone patio framed by fat stone pegs
Placed closely beside one another

At the patio's center was a wooden dining-room table
Set for two with plates and cups of the softest gold
Beyond the patio was a single tree

The tree's ten branches extended away from each other
At the tip of each branch protruded sharp shards of crystal
That surrounded tight bundles of tiny fruits

Beneath the tree circled a lion and lioness
Passing each other, circling within warn paths
These cherubim were terrific specimens of terror:

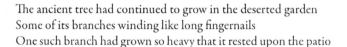

Their eyes were white corneas matching their albino fur
An overflowing mane of blue flame painlessly groomed
The lion's face; blue flames streaked the lioness's ears

The ancient tree had continued to grow in the deserted garden
Some of its branches winding like long fingernails
One such branch had grown so heavy that it rested upon the patio

Shattered crystals and pink lemon-shaped fruits lay at my feet
I picked up one of the soft fruits
Its thin skin was fuzzy

    My teeth pierced its tender pink skin

I swallowed a flood of bitter juice–
My throat burned and swelled
I felt as though I was being strangled

My heart raced faster as a stream of heat crept through me
My muscles quivered and shook
Leaving me upon the patio's stone floor

Tiny blue flames came from my pores
Uniting together as if my skin were paper,
Consuming my body in a blaze

A wavering blue engulfed my vision
I rolled in anguish upon the patio
And the flames vanished

    I calmly rose from the ashes of burned skin and hair

Pushing long curly brown hair from my face
With new youthful hands
Strength pulsed up and down my arms and legs

A great clarity of consciousness consumed me

REFLEXIVE CONVERSATIONS

I felt as though I was chiseled by the hand of God
And born from the womb of a angel

Movement in the trees awakened my young heart
Monkeys began a choir of screams,
Leaping onto the roof from the branches of the tallest trees

Two bright-yellow eyes opened in the trees of the garden

Birthed from the dark shadows came a heavy black feline,
His shoulders slowly rolling with each descending paw
Two long tusks extended from his closed mouth–

They raised, like drawn swords, into the air
As he opened his jaws, flattening his large spotted tongue
And violently hissed

A warm breeze of rotting flesh blew past me

As I turned to run
He exploded through the yard,
Entering the realm of the great tree

A deafening squeal forced me to look over my shoulder
The lion clung to his back
The lioness clutched his throat

Blood spilled into the roots of the tree

Fleeing back into the jungle as quickly as I could
Slashing about in the tight cramped space
I knew I couldn't return;
Not to the Garden of Eden,
Not to Melon Colony

I moved to the other side of the Island of Purgatory

X. MY GREAT ESCAPE

On high vantage dunes,
Where the yellow sands of summer
Balance the going blue of an endless sea

I patiently watched the patterns of the tide

The regularity of the waves
Are like the mothers heart beat
From inside the womb

Such leisure aided the clear-headed sorrow
That followed me like a shadow,
Forcing me to wonder:

I spent long hours in the sun
 Lying out
  Darkening,
   Waiting for each day's open and close,
    Waiting for a particular moment–
    Unknown to me

Watching the tide upon the shore
Thinking of my great Love lost
I longed to return back to the womb
And leave for good the Island of Purgatory

Forcing my way out like an newborn infant
I decided to produce my escape from the inside out
And before the stars and cool of the coming night
I walked down the dunes and left with the good breezes flight

II
REFLEXIVE
CONVERSATIONS

I. THE NAKED COUPLE

When Tomorrow comes calling,
Rising from the land
Like a bright ancient horn
We will rise, like beautiful mummies
Wrapped in white bed sheets
Awakening to the dawn of another life

But she has not yet arrived

So we began talking this night,
Waiting for Tomorrow's dew breath
To be exhaled from her dark slender throat

We asked for silence by striking matches for candles,
Placing a needle onto a turning vinyl record,
Then burrowing our naked bodies beneath soft cotton sheets,
Exposing only our curious looks and pale shoulders

REFLEXIVE CONVERSATIONS

II. FACE TO FACE

She wanted to talk of God and Heaven
And all that she thought awaited us

She closed her eyes and described beauty:

She imagined piercing his cloudy floor-
Gently rising beside white-clouded bluffs
With waterfalls of splashing light
Illuminating her thin soul

She would greet those waiting
In the flushing white-light.
Together they would feast,
Around long beige clothed tables
With golden bowls of black plums
                    Plump purple grapes,
            Crisp red apples,
      Tender green pears,
Sliced pomegranates

They'd drink from simple clay jugs
Filled with dark red and pale-yellow wines,
Laughing together in the shared vision of previous youth
They reminisced about first joys and fears, first dates and tears:

"...Together, after testing the warmed waters of August, he and I
      sank into the beach,
Collapsing into our heated bodies..."

They would leave their feast, to fly and swim,
Silently praising their unseen God
Who set their table like a smiling servant–

        The record player's needle was between songs
        Filling the silence with gentle pops

REFLEXIVE CONVERSATIONS

The Night was still sleeping, her breathes
Blowing even breezes through our opened window
Making the long white curtains tremble

My lover turned to me wondering what I saw of heaven

Like a physician unable to reveal some terrible prognosis
I hid my fate behind her unsuspecting eyes,
And tried to oblige

As *my* mind imagined heaven,
I knew my words would not amount
To a shining kingdom of golden strewn clouds
Where vows were sung
By centuries of angelic choirs

Closing my eyes for personal vision, heaven appeared
Empty.
On my left and on my right
Was both endless day and endless night
Divided by a sandy path:

If I looked left
I watched stars turning in ancient epicycles:
Circles with-in circular paths,
Cutting the sky like glass
With a constant fading trail of flame

If I looked right
I was welcomed by a motionless sun,
Suspended above the cloudy horizon
I could see passive souls (like tiny black dots)
Trapped in orbit

Gregorian chants, in religious hushed tones,
Could be heard far away,
Passively mourning the silence of God

I imagined the heavenly choir:
Several rows of monks
With dark oversized frocks with drooping hoods
Darkening all but the tips of their noses

Their voices sounded distant,
As if carried by a giant cathedral's open-door breeze:

Touching the buttressed ceiling,
Skimming over the cold stone floors,
And up a spiraling staircases,
Leading to heavy iron bells
At rest, because here there is no death

They sung in a dead language:

*"in omnem terram exivit sonus eorum,
et in fines orbis terrae verba eorum... "*

Suddenly, a hand rested on my shoulder.
His voice was warm and tender, speaking softly,
Pronouncing every vowel

*"The cords of the grave coiled around me;
The snares of death confronted me –
My child, they sing these words for your lover"*

My eyes were still closed to my waiting lover
Who watched me adoringly as though I were sleeping
I remained silent about the visions that consumed me

REFLEXIVE CONVERSATIONS

III. THE OPERA OF THE CALM SEA STORM

I opened my eyes –

> My lover was watching me
> Her face tight with awe
> She was lying down;
> Her long black hair across her pillow

The record had ended
So I quietly escaped the sheets,
As not to disturb the sleeping Night.
Finding a new record,
Among a pile of record sleeves,
Called, "The Opera of the Calm Sea Storm"

> White wax slowly dripped down
> The candle's collapsing walls.
> My love craved more;

I produced a long, human-sized painting,
In a frame of frozen golden waves and curls:
A lone ship on a distant sea
Sailing out towards a giant setting sun

> The water was black and dark blue, froth with bronze tips

Notice only one sailor holding the ship's knotted wheel
Sailing off, toward the horizon –
Towards the soft sinking of the afternoon sun
With as many memories as he could carry

She gazed, as one does at a shooting star, at the ships retreat
She dared not blink, for she feared

The sailor with his lone ship would sail over the seas edge,
And out of her sight–
The painted ship remained still

She listened carefully

I painted this during a strange summer night:
Snow silently collected here at my window,
The moon was still and illuminated
All the snow that fell beneath it

This canvas sat before me like a mirror
Inviting me to trace the distant memory
Of my journey after the Island of Purgatory

As the paints dried, I saw what I had become:

A great sail, filled by breezes
That carried me wherever they wished
The Sun's warmth poured over my body,
Sedating me like a drunk,
Forcing me asleep for entire days,

The ocean carried me
As I drifted calmly with a few splashes from the curious water–
The ocean has always carried me;
Carried me away

Looking back to my Love,
I noticed her staring into the painting's dark undercurrent
Showed something foreboding–
Something controlling–
An ocean with cold currents of effect;

She yearned for knowledge of where my voyage began
And so I told her

IV. LEAVING MELON COLONY

My feet squeaked with each step
As I walked down the sunburned dunes
To an absent shoreline
I stood on the damp sands, watching as my feet
Were rinsed by the cold colorless tide.

I entered the water with determination,
Walking till the sea rose to my chin,
Ready to end my suffering
As I prepared to drink all of the sea
A distant trumpet could be heard calling out to me,
Asking me back to Melon Colony,
To live, forever basking in the lazy warmth of its purgatory

Its musical notes drifted in the breeze,
And rested in my mind

But as I turned, ready to return,
I felt the rushing pulse of the cold sea-

An undertow pulled my legs from under me:

I was pulled along the sandy sea floor,
As though I were being dragged by a dark horse
I clawed in vain at the sea's floor
Cutting my hands and fingers on shattered shells

Suddenly the sea floor disappeared from beneath me
Leaving me drifting into darkness
Far above me was the water's bright surface
My feet dangled above blackness

REFLEXIVE CONVERSATIONS

As I began to sink
The water's pressure crushed my chest,
Squeezing my lungs like tender balloons
My cheeks bulged with the last of my air

My eyelids fluttered like a tired reader,
My muscles jerked uncontrollably,
Beads of air escaped my nose-
The ocean was prying open my mouth,
Ready to plunge into my hollow chest

Yet something else was happening:
Heavy vibrations rumbled around me,
My rib cage shook,
My teeth chattered

Staring into the wall of darkness before me
My eyes slowly opened in horror
As a massive blue shadow burst through the darkness
And swallowed me up

V.   THE BLUE WHALE

I awakened inside the dark hollow rib-cage of a giant Blue whale

My body felt defined in dehydration
My mouth tasted of the sea's thick salt
My lungs burned as if they held a flickering flame

I was surrounded in her dark womb
Listening to her calm thick heart beat
I could hear the deep sea's chilled water
Circulate around her as we drifted and plunged

She would surface, during gently falling rain,
Dilating her air hole long enough for raindrops
To tap the walls of my open mouth

I waited for still streams of daylight
To fall through her air hole
And into my cramped space

After a few minutes atop the surface
She would close her air hole,
Sealing off the outside world
And plunge into the heavy darkness

When she fed, she filtered little shrimp and fish
Through her picket teeth,
They washed in and brushed my knees,
Raw and ready to eat

After many months
She surfaced to a bright morning
Speaking only in grunts and red watered groans,

I was gently expelled,
Our eyes met and cried as she slowly submerged

REFLEXIVE CONVERSATIONS

Beyond the reach of light, slowly fading away,
As if in a moment of disbelief;
As if repeating "goodbye" to herself

VI.   THE DRUNKEN CRUISE

As I floated alone, among moving mounds of water
A ship, with limp sails, sat waiting
Leaning from side to side.

A heavy chain led into the blue water
Pulled by the great weight of a solid anchor
I climbed the thick chain onto the deck,
Finding no captain or crew

The ship was full of nets and horse-haired ropes
Washed with white colonial soups.
Lowering my nose to the ship
I could smell the oak forest
That each plank had originated

Climbing atop the ship's crow nest
And lowering my right ear
I could hear the creaky wooden planks
As if they were branches on darkened oak trees,
Stiffly swaying in the breeze

Shading my eyes with a lazy solute,
I witnessed a dark anvil cloud on the horizon
Flashing its distant presence

Climbing down
I quickly reeled in the heavy anchor,
Dripping with drenched seaweed

A massive breath of wind barreled toward the sails
Flattening the waters it passed over
I seized the ship's great wooden wheel
Spinning it fully to its starboard side
Preparing to route the purple-housed clouds on the horizon

REFLEXIVE CONVERSATIONS

Three large masts held the beige sails, now bellied out
Gulping the rushing wind,
Pushing me in a great burst of speed
The ship laid a trail with frothy white wake,
Which faded into the ocean
Heading over the horizon and away from the storm,
I came to belief that fates wrinkled hounds could no longer
    follow me
For my foot steps were erased by the formless water

VII. THE ARCTIC PASSAGE

My ship had sailed gloriously
Breasting every wave with little splash
Splitting the ocean with its rudder

Fate blew against my sails
Thrusting me along the Arctic's black water

At the bottom of the world
The sun never emerged from– nor plunged – into the icy waters
   below it
Only circling the sky in tight orbit

I sailed under the shadows of blue-blooded icebergs
Each floating alone like a cloud at night

I landed once on dark frozen soil
Finding a giant white bear
Laying on his side,

     His black eyes staring blindly,
     Body limp and unmoving
     With patches of fur lifting in the arctic breeze

I skinned the beast,
And unhinged his jaw-
Placing his skull atop my head
Letting his white coat cape down my back-
His large teeth dug into my forehead
His powerful claws dangled at my hips
And dragged at my feet

I thanked the beast for the warmth provided by his coat
And climbed aboard my ship
As a stocky Skua bird picked at the bear's fleshy remains-

REFLEXIVE CONVERSATIONS

I quickly left the frozen land with my crown of teeth,
Watching the land slowly sink into the darkening sea

After two nightless days
The suns orbit widened
Blindly skimming the horizon
My ship climbed north where the waters were blue now
Short chilled breezes were followed by short gusts of warmth

White sails bellied out,
Planked deck creaking and leaning,
I rested on the boats edge through the afternoon
Sailing the whispering winds of reminiscence
Gazing out under the warmth of my bear-toothed crown

VIII. FINDING THE
SYMMETRY OF EROS

My Love remained silent
Looking up from her pillow
Smiling in wonder of me

Soft touches of my finger tips
Follow the natural creases
Of her relaxed body
I can find her symmetry with my fingers
    Which slide down the straight bridge of her nose,
        And over the soft groove above her lips
          I gently cut across her parted lips,
      Tracing a straight line to her tiny chin,
And then slowly roll down her slender neck-

I pull the white sheets off her chest,
Exposing both pale breast

As I was above her
Heat rose from her body, like a soft flame,
Rubbing my chest and stomach

Each warm embrace was new
Each brave collision a triumph;
We discovered love's symmetry
Together.

REFLEXIVE CONVERSATIONS

IX. MEI AMOR IN PACE REQUIESCAT

As the diamond needle rode
The last of the records black grooves,
I watched her

She had fallen asleep
Under the invisible feather weights
That accumulated, like falling snow,
Over her eyes

She goes moments-on-end without air
Swimming around in her open dreams
And then resuscitating herself
With a full unconscious breath

I wonder what images pour past her eyes.
What Garden does she walk through?
What gold and black spotted animal sprints beside her?
What shapes are the shifting clouds she watches
As she lies in a quiet meadow?

The record finished, now spinning silently.
The sky glowed a bluish grey
As Day awakened,
Slowly sitting up on the horizon

Morning birds busily chattered,
Sending their song, with the moist breeze,
Through our open window

REFLEXIVE CONVERSATIONS

Resting my head on my pillow
Closing the curtains of my mind
I let all of my memories rewind
So I can call on them again
Tomorrow.

III

REFLEXIVE CONVERSATIONS

REFLEXIVE CONVERSATIONS

I. THE GREAT HALLS OF JUSTICE

The Great Halls of Justice
A series of white marble arches
Large enough for giants to wallow through

These silent passages echo my hesitant footsteps,
As if the walls were eager to repel every sound,
Sending them back and forth down the open hall

Sunlight enters the large hall
Through large square-openings in the ceiling
Bracing, like beams, against the floor

A single flight of marble steps lines the left-hand wall
Curving around and disappearing
Onto another floor

A cool breeze blows from a smaller arched passage
Beneath the rising marble stairway
The entry way is narrow

Natural light at the end of the passage
Illuminates an adjoining hallway
That continues to the right

Walking through the darkness to the end of the narrow passage
I discover a cloister-like hallway with open doorways
Of warm light lining the left-hand wall

Inside the first doorway:
An open room without an exterior wall;
Only a short marble balcony extending between both sides,

Loosely wrapped in thin vines with tiny pungent flowers,
A sweet mist of honey and vanilla lingers in the air
As if the room were a kitchen of freshly baked pastries

The tops of tall trees reach over the balcony
Dangling ripened fruits and leaves
Large wooden vines wrap the trunks like snakes

This massive palace of emptiness bestows a calmness upon me
I pick a soft fuzzy fruit and rest on the balcony;
Pale-clouded juice falls down my chin

A large golden bowl sits on the rail at the far end of the balcony
Holding the cold water from a recent rain
With both hands, I cup the water and bring it to my face

Laying on my side across the warm marble floor,
And resting my head upon the bicep of my extended right arm
I bathe in a pool of afternoon light

As I lay there, my eyes close easily
The half-eaten peach rests in my right hand
Slowly becoming heavier

My fingers begin to relax
And open;
The peach rolls onto the floor

II. SLEEPWALKING IN THE SHADOW LANDS

I find myself standing in the rolling poppy hills of a strange land
Where the sky is a graveyard of light
Buried in the slow procession of dark clouds

But I am not alone

Above me a winged shadow: A raven glides overhead
Landing beside a flock of ravens perched upon
The creaking branches of an ancient tree, cawing
Alerting my eyes to the cause of the tree's agony:

A man

Dangling from the lowest branch of the dead blackened tree
His face pale; frozen in anguish
Half-open eyes plead for release
From the rope that torques his neck;

Blue unmoving lips

His gaze shifts upon the horizon
As the wind blows beneath his feet,
Pushing over the poppies across the field

REFLEXIVE CONVERSATIONS

III. JUDAS AND JUDGMENT

I awaken to find myself lying across the marble floor
A blue-winged parrot, with his bright yellow chest
Lowers his curved black beak into the flesh of my fruit
And eats it

I move from the room of warm light and into the hall
Continuing down the long passage
In search of the next room
I'm stopped by tall oak doors

I slowly twist a golden skeleton key that waits in the keyhole
Until I hear the slap of wood and metal
Echo into the next room
I heave the hulking doors open:

The cold polished marble on which I stand
Continues into a dark chapel-like room
A series of pillars of gently stirring light
Descend from large openings in the ceiling

In the middle of the room sits an old man in a golden thrown,
Hunched over and silent
His head leaning far over
His eyes closed while he gently heaves

A crown of silver thorns lay crooked upon his skull
Dry blood lines his face like cracked paint
Lifting his weighted head and raising his heavy brow
His sore eyes stare immediately into mine

He began speaking

The sweet fruit of fate summoned you with a dream of me,
Hanging from a blackened tree-
Since that day I was condemned to wait

REFLEXIVE CONVERSATIONS

For the man whose sin would surpass my tragic fate
I've been waiting for you, since before you were born-
Carrying the weight of this silver crown of thorns
Blood has dried in the folds of this ancient frown;
And now I finally wish to escape the weight of this crown-
I was sentenced to be your judge and jury
So please, let us hurry-

Judas halted his speech, lowering his head,
Resting his neck
Closing his eyes
He continued

Now please tell me where you come from, tell me your story,
So I can judge you and be with my father in all his glory

IV. THE CARIBBEAN

After 33 days at sea

Branches and sticks appeared
Floating in the water
Flocks of birds flew overhead

A long tropical island emerged from the horizon
With the morning sun,
Swelling with trees and colors

The wind pushed me closer
I could see the shore:

> White sands gleaming
> In the early morning light

Fish scattered in quick burst
As the shadow of my ship
Crashed over their bodies

Plunging my anchor a half-mile from shore
I prepared to find the most tender fish-meat

I stripped off my white bear-coat and crown of teeth

With only a red sash tied loosely around my waist
And my knife secure between my teeth
I dove into the green aqua labyrinths

> Light scattered like broken glass
> Over my arms and body
> A great green sea turtle slowly glided by

REFLEXIVE CONVERSATIONS

Chasing schools of brightly stripped fish
Stabbing the water in their direction
I pierced one through the middle

I surfaced beside my ship, climbing aboard
With my fish squirming on the blade:

Slowly dying –
Slowly letting go-
Slowly allowing the sun's bright light
To flood its wide eyes

V. THE SHORE

Dark skinned people collected on the beach:
Topless women held their naked children
Young boys and men swam out
To get a closer look

The entire tribe had emerged from the shadows of the trees
Tawny elder men stood with lowered bows
Beautiful women flashed gold earrings

As I neared the beach
Those watching from the water
Swam out to get a closer look

The ship dragged along the shore's sandy floor
As it entered the beach's shallow water;
Gently slowing its speed;
Stopping it just before the beach

Lowering myself down a rope
Into the gentle knee-high surf
A thousand silent faces watched

They saw my crown of teeth nestled into my forehead
They seemed amazed at my bear coat
As it was half-drenched with salt water

Their mouths opened at the shiny knife
Tied against my hip with my red sash

Some came running towards me
With great smiles, and speaking an awkward language
Others retreated back to their village
Returning with balls of cotton and parrots
Fish-bone spears, and glass beads

REFLEXIVE CONVERSATIONS

One child reached for my bright silver knife-
A drop of his blood fell into the clear water

VI.   THE VILLAGE

Their dark eyes clung to me as I stood there on the shore
Quietly looking around

I lunged up the swift incline of the beach
The dark skinned people swarmed around me,
Making deep primitive sounds from their muscular bellies
The younger women touched and groped my arms and shoulders
While the little boys could only look up with smiles,
Stumbling over themselves as they paced beside me
The tribe's men walked ahead of me,
As though they were beating a path
Through the cool empty shade of the tall palm trees,
Hunched over the beach

The village was a dirt-flat of cleared land,
Surrounded by a looming jungle
A series of small wooden huts circled the village,
Women came and went through the dark openings of their huts

The men ordered their children to join their mothers

    Children clung to their mothers' legs

I was brought before a great pit of smoldering ashes
The tribe's men stood to my right, shoulder to shoulder,
And began chanting into the sky

    Skinny dogs cautiously sniffed at my heels

From a short cabin to my right walked a man
With raccoon eyes of black paint
And a beautiful young princess

She wore a head piece of parrot's feathers,
Gold necklaces of varying lengths hung around her neck

REFLEXIVE CONVERSATIONS

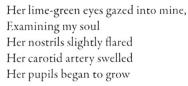

Thin silver earrings dangled from her ear lobes
Her body was covered by the heavy fur of a grizzly bear

Her lime-green eyes gazed into mine,
Examining my soul
Her nostrils slightly flared
Her carotid artery swelled
Her pupils began to grow

I could feel her eyes pull me
Into her–

The man beside her clapped twice

Six young women appeared around me
Placing their hands on both of my arms
Pulling me into the darkness of an empty hut

VII. THE LAST SUPPER

Before a Great fire
I sat cross-legged on a simple wooden platform
Beside the hardwood thrones' of the raccoon-eyed priest
And his princess daughter,
As I had each afternoon since my arrival
Twelve moons earlier

I wore my gown of polar bear fur
Its teeth across my forehead

Shapely naked women brought me food
At their husband's urging:
Bright-yellow heads of corn,
Mashed up yams,
And brown carrot-shaped cassava

Young girls danced around the fire
To the pounding of leather drums
Excitement was shared between the people
As they sang and ate

My six muses danced near me, pulling my attention away from
    the princess
They watched me and slowly surrounded me;
Like a wild encounter with a pride of lionesses

    My heart raced into a callous excitement
    As they approached me

The man with black paint around his eyes,
Danced into the circle from behind me
Wearing a lion's skull as a head piece

He was a holy man;
The tribe's priest,
Petitioning those gods in the sky

With a swift fist into the air he brought silence

He gestured for each dancer to fall to their knees
And bow before me
He stood before me and pulled me up
Lowering his clenched hand to reveal

A large blue topaz gem

Placing it in my hand and closing my fingers around it
He pushed me towards the bowing dancers
Signaling me to give one of them the stone
And, I assumed, make her my wife

Each girl looked up, begging with their smiles for the stone
I walked before each of the young girls–

All had followed me, like a shadow, for the previous year
Tending to my needs:

Gathering wooden-baskets full of fresh coca leaves,
Lowering grapes into my mouth,
Bathing me in hot water springs,
Laying beside me at night, singing soft songs of sleep

However, none of them followed me
Into my dreams
I couldn't pierce their callous stare
I couldn't see through their dark eyes

Each night I disentangled myself from their legs and arms,
Leaving my bed to creep through the sleeping village,
Walking past the smoking ashes of the fire pit,

And over to the princess's small hut

Each night I would peer into the cramped space to find
Her face preserved in moonlight; she was awake
Beneath her shut eyes,
Running from the falling of stars and arrows,
And into my arms

The gem remained in my hand

Finding the princess sitting alone atop her crude wooden throne,
I walked past the last of the dancers and towards her
Standing before her, I placed the light-blue gem into her hands
The stone fell to the earth, resting between her feet
Her face fell forward into her hands
She began to weep

The priest bellowed into the sky and the people swarmed me

The village men hoisted me onto their shoulders,
Carrying me through the village and into the dense forest
I was stretched out atop many hands
(The Vitruvian Man)

I could see the entire tribe follow
As low branches dragged across my face
Their feet smacked against the forest clay

Then, in a rush of sun and wind,
We escaped through a small opening in the foliage
Stopping before a field of Indian Pipes;
The white leafless herbs were healthy and vibrant

Released from the men's bony shoulders,
I stood in the shadow of a tall pyramid-shaped structure
With narrowing stairs that led to a small square temple at the top

REFLEXIVE CONVERSATIONS

VIII. THE TEMPLE

Standing before the temple, at the top of the long stone steps
I could see the village as a small cluster of dark circles
My ship gently rock against the beaches white sands
The sun began its short plunge into the ocean,
Pulling a darkening sky with it

The priest stood between the princess and I,
Holding our hands,
Announcing prayers to the villager's
Who gathered far below us

Releasing our hands
He quickly pulled my polished silver knife from my red sash
And raised it into the sky

After a moment of silence
He pressed the flat-edge of the blade against his heart
As he turned towards the temple and walked in

Following him into the square opening
I entered a hollow room
With a large, circular opening above us

Pointing downward with the knife,
He signaling me to lay flat across the floor
In the eye of the ceiling

I lay there, looking up, like a patient on a table

    Faint stars began to surface

The priest faced away from us, chanting prayers into the wall
The princess stood by my feet,
Turning the blue-gem over in her fingers
 When I smiled at her, she would only look back at her gem

The day's light had completely evaporated
Leaving an enduring clarity to each star

Cool moon light began to enter the room
He pointed to the sky and placed the knife in my love's hand

She looked down at my feet and then up to my eyes
She could see that fear rushed into my nostrils

    The entire moon drifted over,
    Centering itself perfectly before me,
    Like the open eye of God

I was now immersed in cool ghostly light
The priest cocked his head curiously at the princess
And then looked up,
As if to ensure the placement of the moon

My love stood above me like the Shepherd of a single sheep
And raised the knife over her head

    The moon's light began to move over me
    And into the corner of the temple

Her hand fell violently
Resting the knife deep within my chest

    The milky light crept up the wall,
    Moving outside, and back into the night

Her soft lips, drenched in tears, pressed against mine
She closed her eyes, escaping her blasphemy
And slowly released the knife

I stood up and slowly removed the blade from my left breast
The blade was clean

No pain or wound existed
Only the bright noise of the blade
As it fell from my hands
And danced across the stone floor

The priest and princess stood together in the temple's dark
    corner
I realized that it was the fruit of that tree of life
Giving me eternal youth
That protected me from my knife

I looked at my love and turned away
And walked down the steps,
Where a gentle mob expelled me
With opened mouths and eyes

I left the village and entered the jungle's steady hum
Where I walked the entire night
Through a ghostly empire of moving shadows
And reaching plants

When morning arrived
I had escaped the jungle
Finding myself at the beginning of a shallow marsh
At the far side of the marsh was a great island of tall trees

The trees parted to reveal a bright white palace
Rising up like a lighthouse from a bed of weathered marble
Several flights of pearl white steps led to an open entrance of
    towering pillars
I proceeded through the wet grass
Towards the palace

REFLEXIVE CONVERSATIONS

IX. MAN IN THE ROOM

I sat before Judas,
In silence,
Wondering if he heard anything at all

He looked as though he was nailed into his throne
Hunched over the invisible spike lodged below his ribs.
His Neck limp, head down
He broke the silence with a shallow gasp

Each movement was with great effort
As though he struggled against the invisible spike
That pinned him into his throne.
Bracing his forearms against the wide armrest
His body trembled as he hoisted himself onto brittle legs

Hunched over
He raised his shaking hand,
Extending his index finger – pointing at me

"You see, I have chosen to sit right here
Watching months turn to years
Preferring my judgment of waiting in this room
For he whose soul would be exhumed
But it wasn't until you opened those large doors
That I realized they had been locked forevermore
Nevertheless, I still was free
For my will didn't conflict with the walls around me

I could tell from your eloquent defense
That you believe fate renders freedom a false pretense
It is true that we are not free
If by "free" you mean we choose our destiny
Freedom is not found in having free choice

But is found in our desires matching our destiny's voice
My dear boy, we are all caught in a causal web
Where nature's fairness will flow and ebb

We are like the monarch butterfly migrating the earth
Eagerly moving towards a purpose desired from birth
Some achieve their end and pass on happily
Others do not and thus are not free
My boy, you tried to fly,
To fulfill the desires in your mind's eye
You fluttered your orange and black contrast
Becoming caught in a collision of air as you tried to pass

My son, you were lost in the terrible tides of loss
Traversing your fate, like the Butterfly trying to cross
The collision of air already foretold
Arriving here in this palace of marble and gold.
You are the only one who has eaten from the tree of life
A tragic soul who will never escape his own fateful strife
And now for you I must judge
A judgment which I do not begrudge:

You are now forever barred from the holy trinity
For if God is truly '7', then you are now infinity
You will no longer traverse like a vagabond,
Forever wandering away from the Great Beyond
You will inherit this kingdom and sit at this throne
Advising lost souls who find themselves alone;
Saving this lonesome kingdom from every wandering lord
Who has stumbled along their journey and fallen upon their
*   sword*

The judgment floated down the dark passages of my ears
Tickling the tiny hairs of the quiet canals
Gently landing on my eardrums

BOOK THREE

The world beneath me seemed unstable
Darkness clouded my eyes
His voice became a distant echo

The first will be last, and the last will be first
To walk the gently rising path which you once traversed
And cross into the gates of that strange land
Where we walk without feet and touch without hands
You will most certainly be last
As was determined by your recent past
When you happened to eat from the Garden of Eden
You became immortal, wandering the world as Satan

His words began to dissolve in a flood of emptiness
Washing away every sensation and thought
Submerging me in unconsciousness

REFLEXIVE CONVERSATIONS

X. AN ETERNAL CROWN

"Pavane" echoes through the darkness
Lifting the black veil from my eyes

Like a dark cloud moving to reveal the sun
Light expanded into my mind

Sensations trickled back into my body
Giving warmth to my finger tips and toes

Before me was the bright door that I had entered through
Illuminated by the warm light that flowed through the hall

The sounds of distant birds were carried into the room
By the warm wind that wandered throughout the open palace

As I rose to my feet, standing beside the tall throne
I realized that Judas was gone, nowhere to be seen

My head felt weighed down
By the chill of a thin golden crown

To my right: a tall bookshelf extended across the room
One-hundred dust covered books crammed upon the shelves

To my left: a large golden funnel
Projecting each note of plucked strings

And in a moment, the chill of the crown began to fade;
As I felt the warm spark of revelation:

I had so long clung to the steep cliffs of my heart
That any movement seemed impossible

But now I walk freely around the palace
Secure as a hermit in a golden shell

REFLEXIVE CONVERSATIONS

XI. RENAISSANCE

My kingdom was forever alive in the endless season of summer

Each day was a carnival of noise
Resonating from the strange animals
That migrated through the mazes
Of untamed growth surrounding the palace

Each night was a silent requiem for the departed sun
Where a blue moon shined into the eyes of the curious

I became a master of the arts:
Reading ancient books with brittle pages and handwritten text,
Painting large canvases of my adventures,
Freeing ancient heroes from slabs of rock with a chisel,
And mastering colorful languages from distant lands

Yet in the time that slowly drifted passed me
No one disturbed the stillness that rested in my home
Peacefulness rested within me
As I deduced that no soul was lost

I carried on with my life of leisure
Until one day, as I finished a painted memoir of my travel at sea,
A familiar silhouette stood in the doorway
Eclipsing the warm afternoon light

An aura of light clung to the soft rim of her naked shapely body

She moved into the room,
Unblocking the arched passage
Flooding the marble floor with warm light

Fearless green eyes confronted me
Her tiny hands pulled my waist

REFLEXIVE CONVERSATIONS

The tender pink of her lips pressed into mine

My long lost Love,
The bright memory of whom
Blinded me of the faith that was to carry me
Into the Great Beyond

We celebrated in silence,
Exchanging vows with our eyes,
Promises with our lips

Closing our eyes, we fully embraced:
A strange energy stirred in my veins
And suddenly, as if her spirit passed into me,
Feelings of sadness and loss pumped from her heart into mine
She too had waited for me at the edge of the world
Where I had fallen so long ago
Having found me, she was now prepared to wait beside me
Until we could walk together
Over the abyss and into the Great Beyond

But I was now a captive of this kingdom,
A wanderer of this world,
Unable to leave this life

When we opened our eyes
The sadness vanished into the daylight
And I felt as though, even in that brief embrace,
A single eternity had come to pass

Wandering the palace
We found a small room that faced the east
And laid together in the room's bed
Face to face
Talking of God and Heaven
Waiting for the Dawn

XII. DELIVERANCE

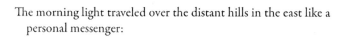

The morning light traveled over the distant hills in the east like a
personal messenger:

> Moving down the valleys and across the land,
> Migrating through the trees of the surrounding jungle,
> Climbing up the palace's eastern wall,
> Silently entering through the bedroom's open window
> And gently awakening us, the naked couple, to our first
> morning

As my lover stood to embrace the new sun
I could see that over night, life grew and swelled in her belly;
I gazed in utter surprise upon this strange blessing:
Our sleeping child, curled up within its mother

Putting both hands on her lower back,
She smiled and left me to myself

Colorful pedals of thought bloomed in my mind
Delivering my open eyes to visions of a son;
One who would fill the palace's great emptiness
And extinguish the fire that gave me knowledge of loss

> The morning light receded away
> As a fleet of dark clouds surrounded the sun
> Capturing its struggling light

The vivid colors of my day dream began to wither;
Each thought was plucked from within me
And scattered into a sudden wind

> A distant flash, frozen in bloom

Entering the hallway

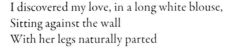

I discovered my love, in a long white blouse,
Sitting against the wall
With her legs naturally parted

Her left hand braced against the floor
Her right hand rested on her heart,
Rising and falling with each deep breath
She peered up, through the open ceiling, and into the darkening
    sky,
As if her eyes were reaching out
Grasping for God

    A broken wave of rumbling rolled high over the palace

Kneeling beside her and placing my hands around her
I could feel her body contract as if thunderstruck

Her white blouse was stretched between both legs
Pooling with blood

Water began pouring down from heaven, crashing into the
    jungle's canopy

The marble hallway became a shallow canal as rain spilled over
The rim of the hallways open-ceiling collected around us
Her body contracted after every few breaths

        The ground trembled from the hard
        pounding of elephants
      Flocks of large colorful birds escaped from
      beneath trees, stirring the air
    Monkeys called out, from high branches, to gather
    their families
  Prides plunged through the wet foliage, sprinting along
  paths only their noses could see
The entire jungle seemed to shift closer to the palace

A small head and arms emerged from beneath the red linen of
    her blouse,
His arms rose up in stiff resistance to the falling rain
That baptized him to this life
His body slowly followed, being washed by the hallway's shallow
    stream,
Oxygen rushed into his tender lungs
And he screamed

The rain stopped

    Rays of light spread over the palace as the clouds dissolved
        into the sun

Gazing up to me,
My Love watched a distant light growing in her eyes
And in taking a deep breath,
She rested her head upon my arm,
Closed her eyes, and fell into herself

I stood up
Cradling her limp body in my arms,
Carrying her down the steps to the front passage,
And out of the palace and past all of the wild animals
That had gathered at our gate
To mourn the loss of their uncrowned queen

My son opened his eyes and the world expanded on forever

REFLEXIVE CONVERSATIONS

XIII. REFLEXIVE
CONVERSATIONS

My son's world rested upon my shoulders,
Growing heavier with discovery each day

He stood beside my statues of David and Adonis,
Believing we descended from some noble race of giants

He wanted to run and play with me,
Walking in my shadow and pretending it was his own

When I sat at my thrown, he ruled from my lap,
Giving mercy to trapped grasshoppers and bees

When he said he wanted to be a king like me,
I would withhold the secrets of my past with a smile

Early one morning, while I studied a new language,
Listening to the piano concerto 21,
I looked up from my throne to discover my son
Standing atop the front steps of the palace

He brought his hands against his hips
And greeted the morning sun as though the palace was his ship
Approaching a bright shining shore

He stood there, crowned by the rising sun,
With my long-lost knife in a dull leather sheath,
Tied against his waist with my red sash

    Loose brown curls cascaded down upon his cupped shoulders
    His shoulder blades flared away from each other,
    Creating a sharp valley down his back

His hamstrings were two taut cords down the back of his
    leg
His calves flowed down from the knee like pulled bows

My boy had grown into beautiful young man
And like an identical twin,
We were now, strangely, impossible to distinguish from each
    other

I watched him as one watches themselves in the mirror;
Intimately tied to the image before me,
Yet separate

My spirit, lingering behind his emerald eyes,
Would always be with him
And when he was to leave,
To cross over into holy eternity,
A part of me would finally be free

As my son turned, moved into the palace, and walked toward
    me,
I saw myself

    Entering the palace for the first time
    Wandering beneath its high ceilings
    Passing through pillars of light
    Towards a fate unknown
As I watched him walk in the shadow of my past
I felt the unbearable chill of uncertainty

    My son now walked a tight-rope
    Stretched between two eternities;
    This world and The Great Beyond—
    So confident in his future
    That he was numb to the whistling wind around him,
    Blind to the abyss below him

Each new step sent tremors into my heart
For each step forward was a step into my past–
And I could not endure a second fall

My redemption rested in his fate
All I could do was advise him and wait;
He stood before me, prepared to confess his intentions to leave

    A Monarch butterfly fluttered passed us
    And glided out an open window

Son,
The freedom I have searched for on distant lands and in others eyes
Is here; first wander your heart, and you will find all that is lost;
Your first journey is into yourself

He merely shook his head, clenching his convictions
As though they were the reins of a ragging bull
I had no choice, but to tell him the secrets of my past
In the hopes that he would stay and avoid becoming lost
In the terrible tides of loss
As I had

So I quickly finished where I left off,
Mastering this new language
With my piano concerto 21 on repeat

Raten…no, riet

Breinigsville, PA USA
14 August 2010
243610BV00002B/11/P

9 781452 060064